TAKE BACK YOUR LIFE

OVERCOME PORNOGRAPHY WHILE BUILDING THE LIFE YOU WANT

BRENDON BYRNE

Printed in the United States of America
Interior Design | www.reneeevansdesign.com
First Edition, 2016

ISBN 978-1-942306-65-8

Brendon Byrne
PO Box 992383
Redding, California 96099

www.BrendonByrne.com

"*Take Back Your Life* unmasks the devastating effects of shame from sexual addictions that destroy connection and intimacy in relationships. Through this book, you will come to understand that the underlying causes are rarely sexual in nature.

If you or someone you love is trapped in pornography addiction or any form of sexual impurity or addictive sexual behavior, this book gives powerful tools and abundant hope for getting free! We are confident that the Lord will use this book to bring about dramatic change in your life as you read it and faithfully do the activations."

BARRY & LORI BYRNE
Founders & Directors, Nothing Hidden Ministries,
Redding, California

Brendon Byrne's book, *Take Back Your Life*, is cold water to the thirsty souls entrapped by pornography and sexual sin. Brendon understands the depths of despair and the hopeless feelings of addiction from personal experience. In this powerful book, Brendon takes us step-by-step down the path to freedom and wholeness as he teaches us how to literally "take back your life." If you have ever struggled with pornography or sexual addiction, this book is for you. I highly recommend it!

KRIS VALLOTTON
Senior Associate Leader, Bethel Church, Redding, California
Co-Founder of Bethel School of Supernatural Ministry
Author of eleven books, including *The Supernatural Ways of Royalty* and *Spirit Wars*

"Today's blazing epidemic of pornography, fueled by the Internet, is in its infancy stages and most are clueless to the cause and effect of its poison. Through candid transparency and vulnerability about his own battles, Brendon not only addresses the problem head on, but he also gives a solid understanding as to why people use porn and how to practically overcome it. This book, free from shame-tactic motivation, is not just a "how to overcome porn guide," it's a life map to learn how to come alive to the world right in front of you."

JUSTIN STUMVOLL
Master Life Consultant, Co-Host of The Liberation Project,
Author of *The Tree Of Life*

CONTENTS

INTRODUCTION

There I stood, a grown man of twenty-eight years, yet never having felt more like a scared little boy in my entire life. I was looking into the eyes of the woman I loved—the woman I had just committed two months earlier to love faithfully and truly until the day I died—and all I could see was the agony caused by my lies and actions. I had promised to protect and love my wife with all I am. I never expected I would be the source of such devastating pain in her life. I could see the pain of betrayal in her broken expression. I could feel the shattering of trust with the person whose trust I valued most, and it made my heart ache. Yet, I had no excuse. I desperately wanted one, but there was no denying or deluding myself about one simple fact: I had chosen hiddenness and deception. I had chosen *porn*.

Pornography is a multi-billion-dollar industry that has flooded our society, and it only continues to increase at an incredibly rapid rate. We have easy access to it wherever there is an Internet connection. And even if we aren't looking at actual porn websites, we are exposed to much of the same soft-core pornographic material through the media—TV, movies, music, magazines, media sites, etc.

Unfortunately, the majority of my generation is being educated about sex by porn, and the consequences may be much more detrimental than we ever thought possible—warped views of sex, addiction, sexual dysfunction, broken relationships and families, harm to the brain and emotional well-being, less satisfying sex lives, and sex trafficking, to name only a few.

Growing up, my education about sex came through media, and starting at the age of fifteen, through porn sites. I continued to use porn into my twenties, largely oblivious to the effects it was having on my life. Then, shortly after being married, my wife found out about my porn habit, and sadly, it wasn't because I chose to come clean with her. Seeing the way this affected my wife and our connection made it clear to me that I had an addiction that I needed to break, and so began my journey to freedom from porn.

Through my process on this journey, *Take Back Your Life* was birthed. My hope is that through this book, anyone struggling with porn will gain significant insight and practical steps that will help them step out of a lifestyle of porn addiction and into a life full of adventure, freedom, and purpose. Each chapter in this book contains vital keys that helped me regain control of my life and move toward freedom. This book isn't just about getting sober. It's about gaining true freedom in all areas of your life, including your sexuality.

As you read through this book you might wonder, *Brendon, why are you putting your "dirty laundry" out in the open for everyone to see?*

Am I embarrassed to share my struggle with pornography, and how I carried my brokenness into my marriage and hurt my wife? Sure I am. It's not fun to talk about my own issues, especially when I chose to keep them hidden until they were uncovered in spite of me. But my embarrassment pales in comparison to the excitement and freedom I now feel. My process of earnestly seeking sexual wholeness has been completely life-changing. What started out as trying to overcome pornography turned into two intense years of the most radical personal growth and development I've ever experienced. After seeing what this journey has added to my life, I will never be ashamed of the moment I said "no" to porn and "yes" to healing and wholeness.

This is why I want people to hear about my struggle. I want others to break the power of porn, shame, and hiddenness in their own lives and begin moving forward toward a life of freedom. I want others to experience God's restoration of everything porn was **I WANT TO SEE A MOVEMENT OF PEOPLE WHO TAKE BACK THEIR LIVES AND FIGHT BACK AGAINST PORN.** trying to destroy in their lives. Most of all, I want each person to experience the *more* God has for them instead of turning to porn, which has no power to satisfy us or bring us love, safety, or any other beneficial thing we need to be healthy and whole in this life. I want to see a movement of people who take back their lives and fight back against porn.

Live with Nothing Hidden

The familiar smell of unwashed jerseys and bleachers filled my nostrils as I entered the gymnasium for my freshman high school basketball practice. As the other guys on the team trickled in behind me, I felt the usual nervousness in anticipation of the difficult workout to come. Every day, our team stretched and warmed up while bantering, trash talking, and joking about the usual topics—classes, our upcoming games, girls, parties, and above all, sex.

When I first joined the team, the vulgarity of the other guys was a shock for me, but I soon got used to hearing about their sexual exploits. It wasn't as if I was completely unaware in this area. I had discovered masturbation, and I would often fantasize and masturbate throughout the week. But the level of sexuality I heard around school was like nothing I'd imagined before. Deep down, I believed it was wrong, but I couldn't deny that my curiosity was aroused and part of me wanted to know more.

On this particular day, the talk ranged from what had happened at parties I didn't attend (including things the guys wanted to do or had done to girls) to "good" pornographic videos they had watched recently. It was hard for me not to mentally picture everything they described.

The arrival of our coach interrupted the illicit conversation and pulled my imagination away from the path down which it had begun to wander. After discussing our performance in the previous week's game, coach put us through an hour of grueling drills. I walked home after practice thoroughly exhausted, only to find an empty house and a note telling me where my dinner was (the rest of my family was off at work or watching one of my brother's basketball games).

As I ate alone in silence, my mind drifted back to the conversations about porn and sex I had overheard at practice. Images began dancing around in my head, giving life to the comments and innuendos made by my teammates. My heart began to race. My insatiable curiosity was piqued, and I was seized by the longing to experience this excitement firsthand. Thoughts began racing through my mind: *You're home alone. You could easily hop on the computer and check out pornography for yourself. No one would have to know. You can finally see what everyone is talking about.*

With my heart pounding in my ears, I found my body moving toward the back room with the computer. I typed the first sexual words that came to mind into the search engine and clicked the top link that popped up. Only a minute or two later, I heard the garage door opening— someone was home. Shaking with excitement and fear, I quickly closed the browser and left the room. Those two minutes had been enough to make one thing certain: I wanted more, and I knew how to get it.

A NEWFOUND SHAME

Once I found pornography, the level of shame and hiddenness in my life shot up to a whole new degree. Growing up in a Christian home, there was an unspoken understanding that anything sexual before you're married is really bad. I already felt shame about masturbating and fantasizing, but looking at porn was on a whole other level of things you *should not* do. I believed there was something wrong with me for wanting to look at porn, and I was terrified of anyone knowing I was looking at it. To cope with my shame, I bottled up these feelings and hid what I was doing. I vowed to myself that no one would ever find out, especially my family, for fear that I would be rejected.

For the next twelve years of my life, I struggled with my conscience and my addiction to pornography. Because of this hidden struggle, my life became full of shame, isolation, loneliness, and disconnection in my relationships. I continually told myself it really wasn't *that* bad to rationalize my addiction, but the truth was, I was silently suffering as porn slowly took over my life.

Unfortunately, the more I used porn, the more I became dependent on it. Even when I wasn't looking at porn, it tainted the way I viewed life. Other activities seemed unfulfilling, boring, and lifeless in comparison to the adrenaline-pumping and overstimulating "high" I experienced with porn. As my need and drive for porn increased, my constant companions of hiddenness and isolation increased as well. I felt more discouraged, scared, lonely, and depressed as the years passed. Even the friends I truly cared about could never know the full me—inside and out—because I refused to come clean about my secret. I was unknown and unseen to the world thanks to my misguided choices.

PORN EXPOSED

The pattern of porn, shame, and hiddenness continued all the way into my marriage. Like so many others, I foolishly hoped that it would all just go away once I got married, but instead, the problem amplified. My wife, Katie, happened to stumble upon some pornographic images on my phone one afternoon. When she confronted me with what she had found, my first reaction was to lie. It was totally ingrained in me to hide anything to do with this part of my life, and I was so scared of what Katie and others would think of me. But I soon realized I had no more room to hide, and the full truth about my porn use came out.

I decided to start seeing a counselor to try to face this giant in my life. Even though I was trying to fight pornography, I still felt hopeless, "screwed up," and "dirty." Soon the craving to look at porn resurfaced. At the beginning of this process, I had agreed to be completely open and honest with Katie about any moments where I was struggling with wanting to look at porn, but because of my old habits of fear and hiddenness, I didn't tell her or my counselor that I was struggling. I silently fought the craving, just as I had done fruitlessly for twelve years, hoping it would go away. Eventually, I caved in and looked at porn again.

By my third session with my counselor, I had looked at pornographic material four to five times in the previous couple weeks and hadn't said any-thing to Katie. I felt horrible inside. I was terrified of the consequences of my actions and yet had no hope that I could change. Despite my great anxiety, I made myself bring up these failures to my counselor. Sadly, I wasn't even completely honest with him. I lied and said I had looked at porn only twice in the previous two weeks. Even while attempting to come clean, I was still hiding. (Shame loves to hide behind half-truths.) After our session, with all the worry and fear my body could withstand, I went home and told my wife the *half-truth* about looking at porn twice in the previous two weeks.

> **SHAME LOVES TO HIDE BEHIND HALF-TRUTHS.**

The hurt I caused to my wife by my deception and betrayal was enormous. Any remaining trust Katie had with me was completely shot. I knew that if nothing changed, I would lose my marriage. This led me to finally be desperate enough to be completely *honest* about *everything*—the one thing I had never been willing to do on my own.

GETTING IT ALL OUT

I knew I had to share my thoughts, sexual feelings, and past actions—all of it—with my wife, close friends, and family. The very thought crippled me with fear. All I could think about was how despicable and unlovable I felt, and how everyone was going to see me that way. Hiding had been my primary strategy to protect myself from rejection. However,

I also knew that unless something changed, I would lose so many more years of my life, and potentially my marriage. It was time to let go of the façade of having it all together and let myself be seen.

Scared and ashamed as I was, I made the choice to begin facing the shame and hiddenness head-on. I got everything out in the open with my wife and those closest to me, and I mean *everything*. I shared things from my past, things I had looked at, and things I was embarrassed about. I also got connected to the Purity Pursuit group here in Redding, California (a group for men who want to live a lifestyle of vulnerability and purity in community), and began sharing with the men in my small group.

One by one, I erased all of my secrets and began living a lifestyle of *nothing hidden*. It was terrifying and yet, there was a feeling of liberation and freedom. I had no idea how much keeping secrets and living a hidden lifestyle was constantly weighing on me until I started living openly. I was so surprised to discover that the more I opened up and let people see the real me, the more I felt loved and known, even when I was sharing my struggles and failures with them.

SHAME-FREE

I wish someone had told me years ago that there is no shame in dealing with a struggle like porn—as long as you face it openly and begin taking steps toward freedom. Shame remains only if you keep it hidden. The lie shame told me, and tells so many of us, is this: "If anyone knows your secrets, they will reject you." I believed it, and so I hid any part of me that I thought might not be accepted. Through my process, I realized that it is impossible to truly break free from anything that we have hidden. Any level of hiddenness, half-truths, or denial will keep us protecting the very

ANY LEVEL OF HIDDENNESS, HALF-TRUTHS, OR DENIAL WILL KEEP US PROTECTING THE VERY THING THAT IS STEALING FROM US.

thing that is stealing from us. But here's the good news: moving courageously past this lie and becoming known breaks the power of shame and hiddenness in our lives.

Believe me, I know from experience how impossibly difficult it can seem to take the first step of being completely honest and open with yourself and those around you about your struggle with porn. But it has been the catalyst that changed my story from one of shame to one of God's goodness and victory. Shame tells you that people will judge you and hate you if they know the full truth about you, but it's not true. The moment I started being completely open in my life was the moment that fear began to break and I saw that people could love me—even the messy parts.

How can you break shame and hiddenness in your own life? The best way is to find someone you love and who loves you, and bring them in on everything that's going on—especially the things you've hidden and felt shameful about. If you don't have someone close, get a counselor or start a small support group (if you need help with creating a group, check out *puritypursuit.com*). The more you choose to be open with those who love and know you, the more shame will break. By coming out of hiding and letting others see the full *you*, you will get to experience love, connection, and understanding right in the middle of your mess and struggles.

Another reason it is vital that we live openly and honestly with others is that it keeps us honest with ourselves. If we let others in on our struggle and it's out in the open for them to see, it makes it more difficult for us to go back to ignoring our issues, pretending they don't exist, or believing they aren't as bad as they seem. It's harder to lie to ourselves and act like everything is okay when those around us know the truth. As frightening as it may sound, we need to remove our ability to hide by choosing community. The simple way to do this is by revealing what is truly happening in our lives with brutal honesty.

Wherever you are in your struggle, begin loving yourself by being open about it. Openness isn't a one-time choice, but an ongoing lifestyle. The benefit of this reaches so much farther than breaking free from porn. Living with "nothing hidden" releases us to live in true freedom with no hint of shame in our lives. It's the best way to position ourselves for continual growth in our personal lives, relationships, and with God. Do yourself an invaluable favor and don't wait any longer. Get open, get honest, and begin taking back your life.

OPENNESS ISN'T A ONE-TIME CHOICE, BUT AN ONGOING LIFESTYLE.

Activation

The goal of this first activation is to remove any and all shame and hiddenness and invite relationships and community in on your process. You will need people around to support you as you continue on your journey of freedom from porn.

Ask God to highlight a safe person to you, perhaps a loved one or a close friend in your community, to meet with this next week. Share with this person any areas in which God wants you to be free of shame and hiddenness—especially the areas of porn and sexuality. Don't be vague; be specific. Allow yourself to be seen and loved in the areas where you believe you are unlovable. Aim to have nothing hidden with your close community. If you don't know how to initiate the conversation, you can try saying something like, "Hey, I have been living with hiddenness and shame for a long time and I know I can't continue living this way. Would you be willing to listen to my story? It's messy but I know I need to start being honest and letting people in if I want freedom in this area."

Take Ownership

There we were, fighting again. The hurt and mistrust were so thick you could cut them with a knife. It had been a couple of days since I had revealed to Katie that I had been looking at porn, and she was trying to communicate how she felt about the whole situation, desperately hoping I would see a need for change in order to restore our damaged relationship. She wanted to be able to trust me and be close to me, but she was telling me honestly that she felt so unsafe to do so. I could hear and see the pain in her every word, and something inside me resented her for it.

Why does she have to be so affected by this? I thought. *Can't she see that I'm trying? Isn't that enough? Do I really have to fix and face everything now?*

I didn't understand it in the moment, but I was mad at my wife for being so hurt because it was forcing me to face the pain of my decisions. I didn't want to feel or own the fact that my choices had caused this great divide in our marriage. So I argued with her. Despite knowing that what I had done was wrong, I was too scared to face it like a man. As she expressed her feelings, I responded with excuse after excuse, continually shifting blame and refusing to take responsibility for the grief I had caused.

Even in that moment, with all my fear and cowardly avoidance, I still greatly loved my wife. It was killing me to feel the disconnection between us, and deep down I longed to feel close to her again, just as I longed for her to feel safe with me and trust me again.

I wanted to believe that, given other issues in our marriage, it was partly her fault that I was looking at pornography. There were some very real communication issues that were making life more difficult in our marriage, but the truth was that I had just as much fault in our communication issues as my wife did, and no matter the communication issues, it was *my* choice to look at porn, lie about it, and hide it from my wife. Outside circumstances may not have helped, but my choice to look at porn wasn't caused by outside circumstances. It happened because I chose it. Period.

ALLOWING MYSELF TO FEEL

After much fear and reluctance, I finally acknowledged to myself and my wife that I was wrong and that I alone was responsible for choosing pornography and bringing it into our marriage. As soon as I did, I felt all my walls and defenses fall. I knew I was doing the right thing by owning my actions, yet all I felt was broken and weak. My attempts at shifting the blame had been my last defense against facing the failure of my choices, and with that gone, my own inadequacy was staring me right in the face.

As I finally allowed myself to feel the full weight of what I had chosen, it felt like my heart was going to break. I was brimming with remorse, regret, sorrow, and just about every other painful emotion you can think of, and yet I couldn't run from them. I desperately wanted to turn off these feelings and hide from this whole mess, but I couldn't do that to my wife. After years of false pride and acting like I had it all together, I was experiencing true humility as I accepted the truth: I was responsible for what I chose and its consequences, which included all the pain my wife and I were going through.

Few things in life are as sobering or painful as being responsible for hurting someone you love. When we've done something that causes deep pain to those closest to us, we often try to make excuses and direct blame away from ourselves. *Yet we mustn't do this.* We cannot grow and separate ourselves from the consequences of our actions if we can't even admit that we chose them in the first place. Yes, it's uncomfortable facing our own shortcomings, but only by fully owning our choice to look at porn can we own our process of getting free of it.

> ONLY BY FULLY OWNING OUR CHOICE TO LOOK AT PORN CAN WE OWN OUR PROCESS OF GETTING FREE.

WITHOUT EXCUSE OR JUSTIFICATION

I can't tell you how many of us miss out on getting free because we hide behind excuses and don't allow ourselves to feel the full weight of our actions. There will always be plenty of excuses available to us:

"My marriage is struggling."

"My job is too stressful."

"I had a rough childhood."

WHENEVER WE GIVE ANY DEGREE OF BLAME TO SOMETHING OR SOMEONE ELSE, WE HAVE JUST ALLOWED PORN TO STAY IN OUR LIVES TO THAT SAME DEGREE.

But whenever we give ANY degree of blame to something or someone else, we have just allowed porn to stay in our lives to that same degree. Do whatever it takes to fully own your problem. Get rid of the excuses. This isn't a very "fun" step, especially if you have been used to living in avoidance and denial like I had been. It is difficult because we are admitting to our own brokenness, but therein lies beauty. As we humbly admit our shortcomings, we position ourselves to receive the help, love, and comfort we really need in the areas where we most need them.

RECEIVING FORGIVENESS

One of the most beautiful things about our God is that if we confess our sin, which means taking ownership for what we did by admitting it, and turn away from it, He will always forgive us. Receiving God's forgiveness is absolutely crucial in the healing process. When I allowed myself to feel the full consequences of my actions, I thought I might break under the weight of it all. It was receiving God's goodness and His forgiveness even when I felt I didn't deserve it that allowed me to continue getting up in the morning and pursuing sexual wholeness. Receiving forgiveness frees us from trying to earn back what we lost because of our poor choices and moves us toward turning away from pornography on a heart level.

Even though God is always faithful to forgive us, sometimes we are so stuck in shame that we can't even receive it. This happens when we allow ourselves to feel the full weight of our actions but never move beyond the heaviness, weight, and pain. Instead of admitting our own brokenness and then going to God to receive His acceptance and forgiveness, we stay self-focused. We get caught in a shame spiral, dwelling on our own inadequacies and ending up paralyzed by feelings of failure and helplessness. We must be courageous enough to feel the full weight of our actions, but we can't stay there. We have to go to God. Experiencing God's forgiveness, love, and acceptance after admitting to our choices and consequences is the only way for us to forgive ourselves fully and break away from the shame spiral.

REBUILDING TRUST WITH OTHERS

Many people don't realize that receiving forgiveness and rebuilding trust are two separate things. Allow yourself to receive forgiveness from God even when you feel you don't deserve it, but know that rebuilding trust with anyone after you have broken it is going to take time. Give those you've hurt time to process. Begin rebuilding trust with your actions, not just your words. Do not make empty promises. If you want to rebuild trust, you will have to be consistent and follow through with what you say.

After months of not looking at porn or masturbating, I

was actively moving forward in my journey toward healing. But there were times when my wife still needed to process through the hurt and betrayal that had occurred months earlier. This would uncover an aspect of something we hadn't fully discussed, or a deeper layer God was bringing up to allow for continued reconciliation. Even though God had forgiven me for my past actions, in order to rebuild trust and relationship with my wife, she needed to be heard and understood as these feelings came up. It was difficult and painful each time I heard how my past actions were still affecting us, but I knew I needed to understand the pain my choices had caused and that these very moments were opportunities to rebuild trust by fully understanding what I had put her through. This is where we need to be humble and understanding, and recognize that healing from our actions will take more than us just not looking at porn and masturbating anymore.

I can tell you that Katie and I now have more trust and better communication in our lives than ever. Your trust can be rebuilt stronger than before it was broken, but during the early stages of your process, give those closest to you time to heal and continually be willing to understand them, even if the pain is from months or years earlier.

REBUILDING TRUST WITH YOURSELF

Not only do we need to potentially rebuild trust with those close to us; we also need to rebuild trust with ourselves. When I first started working on my porn addiction, my trust with myself was so low. I was scared I wouldn't be able to follow through with my own words. My willpower was a sorely atrophied muscle from years of failing after telling myself countless times that I was going to quit looking at porn. I wanted to be a trustworthy person to those around me, but the problem was, I didn't even trust myself. I began to change this by starting to rebuild the value of my word.

Throughout the years, I had made countless promises to myself—to stop looking at porn, to begin working out, to live healthier, to spend more time with God, to quit hiding and isolating, to build better friendships in my life—but rarely did I follow through with any of them consistently. Each time I didn't follow through with these promises, it caused me to lose faith in my ability trust my own words.

As I began thinking about how to establish value in my words, I realized it wasn't going to happen from sitting around and praying about it. I needed actual experiences and successes to build on. I needed to encounter times where I would feel the accomplishment of choosing the right decision in the moment, despite any emotions that were pulling at me to do the opposite. I needed tangible and *clear* goals that would challenge me, but also weren't impossible to accomplish.

I intentionally chose not to make vague or unrealistic goals like, "I'll never look at porn again," or "I will never hurt my wife again." I already didn't want to do these things, yet merely having this desire wasn't enough to help me actually accomplish anything. So I decided to make *clear* and *realistic* goals instead, such as—"I will call someone right in the middle of being tempted to look at porn and not wait till afterwards," or "I am going to be completely open and honest with those close to me, even about what I may think are 'small compromises' in my struggle. I will no longer have any secrets in this area."

After I made these goals, I encountered times when I was being tempted to look at porn and definitely *did not* want to call a friend to bring him in on my struggle. But because I was trying to restore my willpower and my ability to choose what was best for me, along with trying to gain a healthy perspective on sexuality, I would make myself call, regardless of any urges that were trying to convince me to hide instead. Almost every time I followed through with my commitment to my goals, I was so thankful I did, and almost always felt some level of relief from my struggle.

As I began to make the tough but right decisions, I started feeling a little better about myself. I saw that I was capable and powerful to choose even in the difficult moments. I actually took time to think before saying I would do something and ask myself, "Can I commit to this?" I also began to feel glimmers of hope that I actually could change and get free from pornography.

Our willpower to follow through with commitment and goals is like a "muscle" that needs to be strengthened. As this muscle begins to gain strength, we will begin to see a difference not only in our fight for freedom from porn, but in other major areas of our lives, such as our job or career, relationships, personal health, and so on.

If your story is similar to mine, where you've told yourself countless times that you would quit looking at porn and ended up giving in and doing it anyway, then now is the time to begin rebuilding trust in your word to yourself by learning to persist in following through with what you say you will do.

CREATING A PLAN

I completely believe in strengthening our willpower, but we also need to be wise and not put ourselves in situations where there is a high chance of failure to keep our word. Therefore, if we want to see change, we will have to make a plan. I didn't just leave it up to, "I'll try harder," when I knew very well from my **IF WE WANT TO SEE CHANGE, WE WILL HAVE TO MAKE A PLAN.** past that mindset didn't work. So I began thinking about boundaries and behaviors that would help prevent me from falling back into temptations, and I devised a plan for how to continue in sexual freedom.

Think about what you need to do to set yourself up for success and go after it— even if that looks like finding someone to help you come up with a plan if you don't know what to do on your own. Don't just sit back and hope things will change while continuing on with what you've always been doing. Take action and begin moving forward. It is by continued, consistent action over time that we are able to rebuild trust with ourselves and others.

Activation

Create a plan for sobriety. To get sober, we have to begin with stopping the porn addiction cycle, even if it takes drastic limits for awhile until we learn self-control. Be clinical and strict in the beginning. If you need to use an old flip phone or get rid of your laptop for awhile, then do it. Sobriety is not the end goal, but rather the beginning step toward living in freedom from porn. As you gain sobriety, the rest of the chapters on the road to freedom will make more sense.

In creating your plan, you will almost certainly need to do the following:

Engage in **COMMUNITY**, such as a small group, mentor, friends, and/or counselor. In the first months of my journey to freedom, I was seeing a counselor and sharing regularly with my wife about my internal emotions, feelings, and struggles. I was consistently going every week to my men's group, where I was being as vulnerable about my process as I could (which I am still doing, greatly benefiting from, and making into a lifestyle). And I was calling and sharing regularly with my close friends and family, who all knew about my struggle and fight for wholeness in this area. I am no longer seeing a counselor, but all the other areas of community are still thriving in my life today. If you don't develop community around you, you are making the process of getting sober so much more difficult than it has to be.

NOTE: If you want to create a small group but don't know how, check out the men's Purity Pursuit group leader's (Mark Peterson's) book, *Get Naked: A Man's Guide to Great Sex*. His small group model is simple but has been life-changing for myself and many men who struggle with porn. If you are a woman, I would still recommend this book, but you will most likely have to make some adaptations to the small group model.

Implement **PRECAUTIONS AND BOUNDARIES**, such as utilizing porn-blocking software, possibly getting rid of your smartphone or laptop for awhile, and restricting certain websites or social-media platforms.

When I first considered using porn-blocking software on my computer and smartphone, part of me felt prideful. I said to myself, "I want to be strong enough not to look at porn on my own. In order to be strong enough, I need to develop this muscle and learn how to choose not to look at it even when it's available to me. Therefore, porn-blocking software isn't needed." After processing through this feeling with my wife and some trusted friends, I realized that it was actually wise to make looking at porn or sexual material as difficult as possible for me—especially in the beginning. I currently still have the porn-blocking software on my computers and phone as a continued precaution against random links and images that could pop up. My wife is the only one who knows the password to the software, which has worked well for us.

Another boundary I've created for myself is that I don't surf the Internet when I'm bored. I only go on when I know what site I'm going to and why I'm looking something up. This includes social media or video sites. I've found that most of the time when I have a desire to surf the Internet, it is because of feelings of boredom, which, for me, tends to be a trigger for looking at porn. Combine this with the infinite ways to stumble upon sexual material on the Internet, and it just makes it way too easy for mess-ups to occur. I challenge you to do the same thing and eliminate the ways you may encounter sexual content. You may also need to exclude some hobbies, shows, and movies if they are major triggers for you. It is better to be overly cautious, especially in the beginning, while you are learning how to break the harmful habit of turning to porn.

TAKE SOME TIME AND EVALUATE WHAT YOUR TRIGGER MOMENTS ARE.

Evaluate your porn habit and make a **LIST OF "TRIGGER MOMENTS"** when you most commonly want to look at porn. I became aware that there were certain regular times I would be triggered to look at porn, like when I was home alone after work, or when I felt stressed out and wanted to comfort myself. I began listing out these triggers and created a plan for myself so that I was either choosing not to be alone during these times, or to fill these times with something other than porn, such as going on a walk, being around people, or listening to music while resting.

Take some time and evaluate what your trigger moments are. Is it late at night before you go to bed? If so, put a curfew on yourself. Is it right after you get home from work? If yes, then find something else to do after work that makes it impossible for you to look at porn. Is it when you have a project or responsibility deadline and you're feeling stressed? Find a productive way to relax that doesn't involve looking at porn. Especially take note of any emotional triggers like feelings of loneliness, sadness, or boredom. If you're still experiencing difficulty in pinpointing your triggers, the next time you have a desire to look at porn, ask yourself, "What was I feeling or thinking five or ten minutes before this desire to look at porn came up?" Figure out your triggers and set yourself up for success before you find yourself in these trigger moments.

Choose **A FRIEND/FAMILY MEMBER/YOUR SPOUSE TO CALL** when you're struggling to resist the temptation to look at porn. No matter how much you plan and create

BRING SOMEONE IN ON YOUR WEAK MOMENTS.

boundaries to prevent yourself from giving into porn, there will still be times when your desire to look at porn may seem uncontrollable. This is where it is vital to decide that you will call someone right in those moments, *before* you do anything else. The purpose of this is to bring someone in on your weak moments so that you're not alone with the temptation and so they can support you in this process. Instead of only sharing with them that you are wanting to look at porn, be sure to share with them any emotional triggers as well. It might look like saying, "Hey (friend), I just wanted to share with you that I'm really struggling with wanting to look at porn right now, and I think it's because I'm really feeling (lonely, bored, stressed, etc.)." Make a list of some people that you would feel comfortable calling in the middle of moments of struggle and then ask them if they are willing to be these "support" people.

If you are still experiencing lots of failure in your attempts to resist looking at porn, then you will need to revise your plan and keep on trying. Sometimes our plan isn't working because we aren't following through with what we said we would do. If that is the case, you need to ask yourself how serious you are about getting free from pornography. If you are following through with your plan and are still making mistakes, you will need to re-evaluate your plan by focusing on the problem areas and how to improve your existing boundaries. Remember that this is a *process*. Don't get discouraged if you don't get it right the first time. If you are really experiencing difficulty, talk about it with a close friend or family member and find a way to move forward.

> NOTE: If you want to reconcile and restore connection with someone you may have hurt through your porn habit, get the Nothing Hidden Ministries mobile app or tool booklet and practice using the Listening Exercise with them. Once they've felt heard and understood, ask if you can use the Reconciliation Tool with them. These two tools will help guide your communication to begin restoring connection. This isn't a one-time thing, but a lifestyle that will need to be developed.

Facing Your Pain

3

Slowly I dragged myself from the coffin of my bed, still trapped in a waking slumber. The shadows of my lonely apartment were begging me to go back to sleep, but I had hit my snooze alarm more times than I could remember and needed to start moving or I would be late for work. My eyelids felt like ten-pound weights as I squinted around, frantically trying to find clothing. With barely ten minutes to spare, I hurriedly brushed my teeth, grabbed an apple, and ran out the door.

I trudged through my workday with lukewarm interest in what I was doing. The tasks in my position required the intelligence of a bright toddler, and my mind drifted aimlessly as my body automatically performed its duties. I pored over the topics of choice in my head—girls, video games, movies, TV. Once those became boring, I attempted to joke with my fellow employees—anything to keep my mind distracted enough to get me through the monotony of the day. Finally, my "daily sentence" came to its end. I packed up my things, said goodbye to my coworkers, and headed home.

After work, I spent lethargic hour upon lethargic hour playing video games and watching TV, with pornography breaks sprinkled in. After hours of entertainment and staying up much later than I should, I watched some more TV in bed, then masturbated to finally put myself in a comatose stupor that enabled me to fall asleep. A few hours later, the same routine began all over again.

Such was my life as a single guy out on my own. In my mind, I was living however I wanted, but the truth was I was living as a slave, trapped by my own fear of pain. I chose to live in this hellish, meaningless existence day in and day out, all for the sake of one thing—to avoid the feelings that came up when I wasn't pumping myself full of distractions. On the rare occasions when I sat alone with myself and actually felt the emotions my self-induced entertainment coma was keeping me from, I could only discern emptiness and emotional pain. I was so afraid of facing this pain that I continued to drug myself on entertainment, pornography, and any other distraction that would keep me away from deeper awareness. There was no depth in my life, no major growth—only a haze that carried me from day to day, as precious time and life slipped away.

PAIN HAS A PURPOSE

Pain is a very powerful emotion, and not a pleasant one at that. Yet it serves a very important purpose. It indicates that something is wrong, which encourages us make a change in order to stop what's causing the pain. If we never experienced pain, how would we know to take our hand out of a fire before it did permanent damage? If we couldn't feel the emotional pain of loneliness, how would we be aware of our need for connected relationships? Pain is a roadmap telling our body and emotions that something isn't right, and because God made it uncomfortable, it helps motivate us to do something about it.

PAIN IS A ROADMAP TELLING OUR BODY AND EMOTIONS THAT SOMETHING ISN'T RIGHT.

Unfortunately, many people get into the habit of numbing and avoiding their pain instead of listening to it and choosing an alternate course. Emotional and physical pain can be so distressing that we develop a fear of feeling it, and do whatever we can to prevent ourselves from feeling pain. We self-medicate with all kinds of things—porn, food, entertainment, sex, drugs, religion, work, social media, you name it. People use just about anything to avoid feeling pain.

This was certainly true of me. I was terrified of my pain. My life was no longer about living and thriving but about avoiding and numbing. I was hooked on filling my life with anything that helped me get through the day without facing how empty, lonely, or depressed I felt, among many other negative emotions. I was putting myself in a cycle that made it impossible for me to be at peace and enjoy life.

Pornography was one of the strongest and most addictive things I employed to avoid pain, but I knew if I was going to get free, I wasn't just going to have to give up pornography. I was going to have let go of the other things I'd used to self-medicate. After years of using pornography, video games, TV, and books, the thought of letting go of them was like letting go of my dear friends. They were my comforters and my protectors. Yet I knew if I didn't release them, I would only continue running from pain and numbing my life away. So I decided to bite the bullet and relinquish all the ways I avoided pain—what I call my "fillers"—and calm my life enough to find out what truly was going on inside myself. I forced myself to face my inner demons.

GET DESPERATE AND TAKE THE RISK

It can be extremely scary to let go of the comforts and fillers we've used to avoid dealing with our pain. But if we want change, that's exactly what we have to do. This allows us to detox from all the distractions with which we've inundated ourselves to prevent us from dealing with our true issues. We need to get desperate and take the necessary steps we've been avoiding. What does it look like to get desperate? It's getting to the place where you say, "I'll do whatever it takes to get well, even if it means letting go of comforts I've used for years," and backing it up with action. Are you in that place? Are you able to let go of your fillers and distractions to face what's really going on inside you?

Something happened when I cut out all the fillers that had been distracting me from my problems. I began to feel everything that I had numbed for twelve years, and let me tell you, it was not pleasant. Throughout my day, I would randomly get hit with massive feelings of self-hatred, shame, inadequacy, fear, hopelessness, and other distressing emotions. I would have almost uncontrollable urges to go watch a movie, play a videogame, or go look at porn—anything that would distract me from facing these feelings. Despite these urges, I chose to face my pain and began forging forward, slowly gaining ground.

MAKE ADJUSTMENTS

You may be thinking that this does not sound like a healing process, but each time I chose not to numb out and felt depression, loneliness, boredom, self-hatred, or other negative emotions, I was able to make a change in that moment to deal with those emotions. If I was feeling lonely, I made myself pursue relationship with my wife or a friend. When I felt self-hatred, I would call a friend and have him speak God's truth over me, since I couldn't hear it for myself in those moments. When I was depressed, I would pray and begin focusing on what I am genuinely thankful for in my life. For the first time in my life, I was actually listening to my painful emotions and making necessary changes. Instead of doing everything I could to avoid pain, I began to associate positive change and hope with facing my points of pain and finding actual solutions to them. I was taking care of my emotional wellbeing, and as I did, my need for fillers began to lessen.

As we face our pain, we get back something very important we lost while living in avoidance— self-awareness. With *self-awareness* comes the hope for change. When we choose avoidance, we don't know what is wrong, but when we

KNOWING OURSELVES ALLOWS US TO MAKE ADJUSTMENTS AND STOP PERPETUATING WHAT IS ADDING PAIN TO OUR LIVES.

are able to be fully present with ourselves and face our

emotional state, we become aware of what's really going on inside ourselves. Knowing what is going on physically, emotionally, and spiritually inside ourselves allows us to make adjustments and stop perpetuating what is adding pain to our lives. This self-awareness will be especially useful for practicing personal reflection in the middle of temptations (I'll discuss this more in the next chapter), which we won't be able to do if we are still numbing and avoiding pain.

BREAK THE CYCLE

If you are serious about dealing with porn and brokenness in your life, you need to get serious about cutting out any fillers you are using to avoid pain. If you simply replace porn with food, alcohol, entertainment, or whatever else, you have only substituted one addiction for another and won't be able to make the necessary adjustments to stop perpetuating the pain. The consequences may look different, but you are still living in bondage. Don't try to numb, dilute, or avoid your pain—*face* it. Pretending it's not there doesn't make it go away. Burying it deep inside only makes it a companion that silently affects you until it finally bubbles to the surface. It may be extremely difficult, but learning how to move through your pain instead of running from it or avoiding it will propel you forward in your recovery process.

Activation

Take a look at the ways you are spending your time and write out a list of all the fillers and distractions you use to avoid dealing with pain and hardship. Cut out fillers that are perpetuating avoidance and begin the difficult but necessary process of facing what's really going on. The benefits you will gain from doing so will completely outweigh the bondage, masked by the false comforts, that you'll be giving up.

Create regular times to process your emotions, feelings, and triggers from the day and week. I used to take 20—30-minute daily walks to process with God whatever I had been feeling—loneliness, fear, inadequacy, etc. Others like to journal or talk with a friend. Find something that works for you, as long as it's every day for *at least* ten to fifteen minutes. This will help you become more aware of your emotions now that the distractions are gone. Remember, when painful emotions come up, they are a helpful indicator that you need to make an adjustment, not something to avoid.

What's Behind Your Temptation?

I had been sober and living with nothing hidden for about four months. It was a beautiful sunny day, and I was on an afternoon walk, soaking in the wonders of the blue sky above while having my usual dialogue with God, recapping recent events in my life and processing them with Him. Then I noticed a woman walking down the path toward me. I couldn't even see the woman that clearly, but it didn't matter. My palms got sweaty and I could feel my desire to be noticed by this random woman growing.

On cue, my body reacted without any permission from me. I felt a rush of adrenaline surge through me as my heartbeat quickened, and a longing for this woman to notice me began to swirl in my mind. My emotions were telling me I had a desire for this woman, while my mind was beating me up—*I can't even walk down the street and not be tempted! What is wrong with me?!*

I continued walking in a state of semi-shock and anxiety over this unexpected temptation. I couldn't think clearly while my own thoughts of failure and shame, mixed with this carnal drive, were both yelling in my ear at the same time. It wasn't until a couple minutes after I passed the woman that I calmed down enough to remember

INSTEAD OF BEING AFRAID AND AVOIDING TEMPTATIONS, YOU NEED TO FACE THEM AND INVITE GOD INTO THE MIDST OF THEM.

something I had heard from my men's group. Instead of being afraid and avoiding temptations, you need to face them and invite God into the midst of them. This helped me gain some clarity of mind, and I began examining what was actually behind this temptation.

I started with the most basic question: What was my temptation? My answer was that I felt a desire to look at this woman's body (especially her butt and boobs), wanted to feel a sexual connection with her, and wanted her to want me back in the same way. It felt very physical and sexual, not relational at all. I didn't justify or make excuses for what I was feeling, because I wanted to get it fully out in the open so I could begin to face it.

My next question: What was my temptation trying to make me feel? As I asked myself this question, I realized the thought of having this random woman notice me and want me sexually was attached to feelings of excitement and adventure. So I asked God, "Why? Why does thinking about this woman in this way equate to excitement and adventure?" I felt God answer me and explain to me how a large majority of my life I had been sexualizing women through fantasy, masturbation, and pornography to fend off boredom—a counterfeit source of excitement and adventure. Since removing porn from my life, I was now yearning for something thrilling, and my natural reaction was to sexualize women.

There it was, the root I was looking for. I wasn't just some broken and shameful man; I was longing to feel excitement. I wanted to feel alive, which was a good healthy desire to feel, but I was reverting back to my conditioning from pornography to try and meet that need with sexualizing. As soon as the understanding came, I felt the shame drift away and I saw purpose. God was talking to me about my heart and my needs.

I prayed to God and repented for using sexualization to fend off boredom in an attempt to meet my need for excitement and adventure. I asked God to show me how to meet this heart need in a way that was healthy and satisfying—in the way He intended it to be met.

If I hadn't had the courage to face my temptation and process it with God, I would have continued on my way in shame, believing I was just a messed-up pervert who can't control my sex drive. I would have never learned what was really going on behind the temptation.

GETTING TO THE HEART

Through my personal experience of getting free from porn and helping others who are struggling with porn, I've learned that about 90% of sexual temptations have nothing to do with our actual sex drive. They have to do with our heart. They are either the result of desires we are trying to fulfill, or, as I addressed in Chapter 3, pain we are trying to avoid using sex. A common quote we use in the Purity Pursuit group is: "Pornography

> **BEHIND OUR SEXUAL TEMPTATIONS ARE LEGITIMATE, HEALTHY NEEDS ATTEMPTING TO GET MET.**

is a legitimate need fulfilled in an illegitimate way." This means that behind our sexual temptations are legitimate, healthy needs attempting to get met—needs like intimacy, adventure, taking risks, comfort, love, security, etc. What most people don't realize is that these needs are inherent in every human being and when they aren't met in a healthy way, we will often turn to a counterfeit, such as porn, sex, and other fillers to try and get them met. Because these counterfeits will never truly satisfy, we feel the pain of this unfulfillment, and will most likely enter a cycle of continuing to use counterfeits to numb the pain of unfulfillment while repeatedly trying to get our needs met. This is why it can be so difficult to let go of pornography. There is a whole gamut of needs we are trying to meet through unhealthy sexualizing, and when we learn to stop avoiding pain and numbing ourselves, we actually begin to feel the pain of ignored, legitimate needs screaming in our face.

DON'T FEAR TEMPTATION

Contrary to what may be our most natural reaction, the key to finding and meeting our legitimate needs is to look at what's behind our temptations to find the root of what is going on. Unfortunately, we usually miss this step because we are too afraid to admit we have a temptation in the first place. It's common for us to feel that if we are being tempted, we have already failed. This is a lie we cannot tolerate if we want to get free from porn. We will be tempted throughout our life with many different things. The goal is to be able to look at these temptations, recognize what our heart is actually looking for, and then go to God to learn how to meet it in a healthy way. Jesus was tempted in all things and was without sin. Why would we expect to live a life where we are never tempted, when Jesus, who was perfect, didn't even live like that?

The reason we have temptations in the first place is because our heart is crying out for something and doesn't know how to meet it yet. This is what shame is trying to keep you from realizing. You aren't messed up. You are God's creation, and He is a magnificent Creator who doesn't make mistakes.

I've come to realize that the most destructive consequence of temptation isn't giving into it; it's learning to fear yourself, coming to believe you are perverse, and never finding out the truth behind your temptations. Don't give into shame and run from what's going on. You will find keys to your freedom in the sexual pulls and temptations when you bring God in on the process.

That day I chose not to fear temptation completely changed the way I battled porn and sexualization. I started facing my fears by looking at exactly what was tempting me and what need I was trying to meet. If I felt a sexual pull, I would stop and ask myself, "What need is this sexual pull trying to meet? Is there any pain I'm trying to avoid? What am I feeling in this moment? What was I feeling shortly before this pull or throughout this past week?" When I asked myself these questions, I was amazed to discover how many different core needs I was attempting to unhealthily meet—a desire for love, self-value, acceptance, comfort, confidence in feeling like a man and even practical needs such as rest, sleep, and food. I also discovered many uncomfortable feelings that I was attempting to avoid— boredom, stress, anxiety, and fear. Just about any need or pain had the potential to manifest as a sexual pull or temptation.

As I got to the root issues and needs behind my temptations, feelings of hopelessness that I would never change and the shame of my temptation fell away and were replaced with clear steps for how to move forward. For example, if the root issue was that I wanted to avoid boredom, I would repent for trying to meet this need in a harmful way, then pray, "God, help me to learn how to risk and experience adventure with the passions that You've placed inside me." Then I would find realistic ways to "go on an adventure" by taking risks and facing fears in my life. If the temptation was originating from a desire to feel valued or loved, I would pray, "God, help me to see myself as You see me and receive Your love for me, not from other women or sex." Or, if I was wanting comfort from stress, I would pray, "God, I want You to be my Comforter, not porn or sexualization." Then I would go somewhere quiet and connect with God until I felt my stress decrease. And if a temptation was there because I was physically tired, I would make sure I got a good night's sleep.

If you have a tendency to believe you are messed up or perverted when struggling with temptations and you want to break that lie, then you need to choose not to fear your temptations and invite God in on the true desires behind your sexual pulls. Through this process, you will end up learning about yourself and discovering firsthand that your heart is pure and good, even if you don't yet know how to meet your needs in a beneficial way. Begin loving yourself by recognizing the needs God has placed within you, while allowing Him to teach you what to do with those needs.

Depending on how long and how deep our sexual addictions go, our temptations can be pretty gnarly sometimes. I know we want to ignore them and act like our grossest and most embarrassing temptations don't exist, but all I can say is, don't steal an opportunity from God to allow Him to teach you about who He has made you to be. God can use anything if it is completely submitted to Him in a humble and honest way. Even our gnarliest and most shameful temptations can be redeemed by God if we allow Him to show us what's really going on in our hearts.

NOT EVERY THOUGHT IS YOURS

While it is critical that we find the truth of what is going on behind our thoughts and temptations, it's important to note that not every thought is a reflection of our heart either. Sometimes, random sexual thoughts or feelings will go through our minds, but they will only become a temptation if we choose to entertain them. We need to practice deciphering which thoughts are attached to our hearts and which are random. Otherwise we will end up taking ownership of *every* little sexual thought and feeling, putting time and energy into fighting something that may not even be an actual sexual pull.

Usually, if the same temptation is recurrent, then it will most likely be connected to some part of your heart that you will need to process through. Or if you feel a strong emotional pull toward something, that usually means there is a heart need or desire somewhere underneath the pull. But, if the temptation or thought is simply something that popped into your head and you don't feel strongly attached to it, don't take ownership for it right away. As soon as you are conscious of thinking the thought, simply let the thought go and allow it to move on. I tend to try this option first to see if it will just go away. If it keeps coming back or I feel like I really want to give into the temptation, then I go through the process of trying to find out what's going on in my heart.

Many times, once someone has been sober for around one to three months, a lot of pain and issues get stirred up. At the three-month sober mark, it felt like every day was a war zone in my head. On the harder days, it was difficult for me to go a whole minute without something sexual popping into my mind. Don't get discouraged! It is actually a good sign that you aren't numbing pain or uncomfortable feelings and that these are being brought up to the surface. Continue to practice deciphering which temptations you need to face and hear God's truth on, and which ones aren't even yours. As time goes on, you will get better at being able to differentiate which thoughts are attached to actual needs and which ones will only become a temptation if you dwell on them. As a result, the frequency and strength of the temptations will become less and less.

If you are having a difficult time in this process, be encouraged that you are most likely doing something right!

Continue to bring God and others in on your struggle. Remember, the only way we don't improve is if we choose to give up and stop taking steps forward.

THE ONLY WAY WE DON'T IMPROVE IS IF WE CHOOSE TO GIVE UP AND STOP TAKING STEPS FORWARD.

WHAT TO DO WHEN YOU GIVE IN

In your journey, there will potentially be times when you give into temptation, even if it's just a little bit. It is important to take even these small compromises seriously, because if ignored, they will stunt your growth process and will most likely open the door to feelings of shame, hiddenness, and isolation again.

If shame does creep in after giving into a temptation to whatever degree, remember to find someone you trust and let them in on what's going on. Even if you haven't given into a temptation, you may still have shame about having a temptation in the first place. Again, find someone to process the temptation with and let them in. Throughout this whole process of healing, we must continue to practice living with "nothing hidden."

Getting free from porn is a *process* and it doesn't happen overnight. Be quick to admit when you make mistakes, evaluate those mistakes, and plan a way to improve and grow in the future. Taking ownership and having a humble, repentant heart are key during this process.

Activation

Pay attention to the feelings, emotions, fears, etc. that are coming up now that the fillers have been removed from your life. Invite God in on this process. Every time you are tempted, instead of running from it, face it by bringing it to God by asking these questions:

- What is my temptation?
- What need am I trying to meet, or what pain I am trying to avoid with this temptation?
- God, how can I meet this need in a healthy way that actually satisfies?

At the end of each day, go through the temptations you had and write down the answer to each of the questions above. As God gives you positive ways to meet your needs, make sure you set aside time to actually do what He told you. The answers you hear from God carry power, and you can stand on them if a temptation keeps trying to come back. Share these experiences with your close friends or community you've invited into this process.

Dealing with the Past

It was a hot summer night and my wife and I were driving to Walmart to pick up some household items. With hands intertwined and genuine smiles on our faces, we breathed slow and grateful breaths as we passed street lamp after street lamp. We had just finished having a long emotional talk in which we had both worked hard to communicate well, and we finally felt truly understood by one another. With this deep satisfaction of connection and love restored, it was impossible not to look forward to spending the rest of the evening with the beauty beside me. As we parked and exited our car, I was brimming with contentment. I didn't think anything could ruin my current mood.

As we moseyed around the store, we passed other women who were uncomfortably noticeable to me. Everywhere I looked there were low-cut shirts, tight butt-revealing leggings, or trashy clothing that drew attention to their bodies. The first couple of women I saw, I was careful to control my eyes. The urge to stare at their bodies was manageable, though I was a little disappointed at how strong it felt. My discouragement grew as the urge increased with each passing minute. With pure focus and concentration, I did my best not to indulge in it, but it was an act of willpower and not one of freedom.

As we purchased our items and left the store, I felt a level of defeat and hopelessness. I had experienced those urges before, but there was usually another reason or need I wasn't getting met that amplified those feelings. This time it seemed like I was genuinely in a good place and couldn't figure out why the pull was as strong as it was. I had just been open with my heart, and felt understood and deeply connected to my wife. I was in a great mood, and out of nowhere, it seemed, these temptations were hitting me like a train.

Slightly embarrassed, I shared with Katie on the ride home the difficulty I had while in the store. Thanks to my wife's incredible patience and understanding for me in this area, instead of getting annoyed or angry with me, she began asking questions and helping me discover what was truly going on. As we processed together, it didn't feel like there was any immediate pain I was trying to avoid, and I couldn't think of any unmet needs I was feeling. Pushing aside the little lie that began creeping into my mind—*See, you really are messed up and there's nothing you can do about it*—I continued to try to discover what could be the cause of this temptation.

Katie and I finally felt like we were getting somewhere when I asked myself the question, "What do I believe I would be receiving from those women if I gave into my emotions?" The answer that came to me was this: They felt safe and accepting, and like I would receive free love without any risk. While I was relieved an answer came to mind, it didn't quite make sense me. I couldn't understand why these women—most of whom looked depressed and broken down—would feel like love and acceptance to me. So we dug further.

THE REALIZATION

My wife suggested that I ask God why I had these strong feelings attached to these kinds of women, so I did. Immediately, God began revealing to me past memories, experiences, and beliefs that had occurred all throughout my life. Within each memory, there was a common thread of not liking myself and wishing I was someone else. I believed who I was wasn't good enough or capable enough and that I was going to be rejected. Interestingly, many of these memories occurred before I ever had a porn issue. For example, even as I went through puberty, these beliefs carried over into how I related to women. I felt so insecure that I wouldn't be "man" enough for a woman or know what to do in a relationship. Most of all, I was so afraid of trying my hardest and still being rejected, which felt like the final blow that would prove all my fears and beliefs true once and for all.

I realized that this issue was deeper than just some stressor from my week or an unmet need trying to get met. I had been battling these fears and beliefs for most of my life, and they were simply manifesting in my sexual struggle.

When I saw this deep-rooted fear of not being enough for a woman, it made sense that I would see a woman who seemingly had low self-value and was willing to offer her body to me as an opportunity for me to experience connection without the risk of rejection. In my unconscious mind, a hurting woman would be less likely to see my own fears of being inadequate and accept me out of her brokenness. I knew and understood how wrong this was in my head, but according to my feelings, it still felt like I longed for those women.

SEEKING HEALING WITH GOD

PART OF GETTING FREE SEXUALLY INVOLVES SEEKING HEALING IN THESE AREAS OF PAST WOUNDING.

All of us have deep-rooted issues that stem from the traumas and belief systems of our past. Part of getting free sexually involves seeking healing in these areas of past wounding. In the previous chapter, I talked about recognizing the needs behind your temptations and learning how to meet them in healthy, legitimate ways, but these deeper-rooted issues often go beyond our unmet needs. They surface because of lies we have believed about who we are. Many times we are unable to see these issues because they have been a normal part of our lives for so long. And even if we are aware of our issues, we can feel at a loss to create a whole new belief system and lifestyle when all we've known is what we've grown up with.

While there are tools and exercises that can help in dislodging these false identities, ultimately we cannot create this change solely through our own strength. We need to seek God in these areas. He knows the timing and next steps to bring about healing and wholeness, and will guide us even when we are unaware of His handiwork. What God needs from us in return is the strength to follow Him into potentially painful past experiences and trust that He is taking us through a process of healing, even when we can't yet see the end result.

As much as we wish they could, some issues cannot be resolved instantly. Even after discovering the root behind my temptation at Walmart and praying and seeking God for healing, in the months to come I still felt a similar pull toward the type of "broken" women I saw. I would brace myself for these encounters, and even though I knew exactly what was going on, the sexual pull was still there. Knowing what was behind that pull did make it easier for me to manage and prepare for situations that might have blindsided me in the past, but I knew the sexual pull itself was only a symptom and wouldn't change unless I dealt with my self-value and fears of not being enough. The attraction I felt for the women who appeared to have lower self-value wasn't going to change unless I dealt with the root cause.

UNDERSTANDING WHERE THE BELIEFS CAME IN

To get healing from a false identity and lifelong belief systems, it usually helps to first understand when and where we developed them. As my fear of failure and not being enough came to the surface, I knew God was saying, "It's time to work on this issue." Any time I felt those fears rise up in my day-to-day life—which was pretty often once I became more aware of it—I began asking God how these fears first came into my life. I discovered that the majority of these beliefs began rearing their ugly head early on in my childhood and especially took root in the dynamics of my relationship with my father.

My father and I have very different personalities. My dad

is practical, analytical, logical, straightforward, and driven, while I am more imaginative, tender, emotional, and easy-going. We both loved each other, but didn't know how to connect on a deeper level very well. Along with our natural differences, my father struggled with anger and frustration throughout my childhood and teen years. I didn't realize it at the time, but every time my dad would become frustrated with me, or even when he was frustrated at something else while I was around him, I would internalize his frustration, thinking that I was the sole cause of his annoyance and anger. Even though much of the time this wasn't even true, to my seven-year-old self, the emotions I felt made it feel very true to me. This especially came out when helping my dad with fixing the car or doing yard work. I would often unintentionally make mistakes and feel the frustration I caused him. I began thinking there was something wrong with me, that I should be more like him. I thought my imaginative and tender side made me "less than" in the areas of life that really mattered. Along with this, I would compare myself to my three older brothers and how they received approval or praise in ways I didn't, which only furthered my belief that there was something wrong with me.

Through these experiences, I began to develop an identity that wasn't how God or even those around me saw me, yet I mistakenly adopted it for truth. Because I thought I was the cause of my father's frustration and anger, I thought I was unlovable whenever I did anything wrong, and since I often messed up with little things when I was just being myself, I concluded that there was something wrong with the core of who I was. I completely missed the positive aspects of how I was different from my father and only saw them as something to be ashamed of. My only way to make sure I didn't make mistakes was to steer clear of risks and anything that made me feel inadequate. Of course, this only perpetuated my inability to overcome fears and strengthened my dread of failure. As God continued to help me understand my past, I could even see how my strong aversion to facing my fears of inadequacy and failure made it that much easier for me to enter into an addicting lifestyle of masturbation and pornography.

CREATING A NEW MINDSET

It felt wonderful to finally begin understanding myself in these areas, but I still needed to learn how to break the hold that the beliefs "I'm not enough" and "I can't fail or I'll be rejected" continued to have over my life. Breaking that hold required a two-front battle.

One front was the past, where all these memories and false beliefs first came up. As God revealed the origins of each lie or belief that had hindered me, I would repent for joining with those mindsets and forgive anyone who helped reinforce them to me. I then asked God to speak His truth to me to replace those lies, and listened until I heard from Him.

Here's an example of what this practically looked like. One time when I was processing with Katie, I was feeling a fear of failure related to a work issue that had come up because I was stepping into a new area in my job. However, my fear seemed disproportionate to the size of the issue.

This kind of discrepancy is usually an indicator that the current issue is just a trigger of an unresolved past issue. So I asked God to take me back to the memory where this gripping fear of failure first came into my life.

What came to mind was a memory of my father teaching me to use the weed-eater. Every time my dad would hand me the weed-eater, I couldn't operate it very well, so he would have to take it back and show me how to use it again. It seemed like a fairly innocent memory, but I asked God, "What lies or faulty beliefs came to me through that experience that I'm still believing today?"

As I listened, I realized that every time my father took back the weed-eater, it felt like I wasn't good enough, and that it wasn't okay to fail or be messy while I'm learning something new. That was exactly what I was feeling while stepping into this new position at work. I was scared that I had to be perfect as I accepted this new responsibility and that it wasn't okay for me to be messy or have a learning process. The beliefs I adopted when learning to use the weed-eater were still affecting me as a grown man.

I then asked Jesus if He would come be in this memory with me and speak His truth to me. When I did, I saw a picture in my mind of Jesus using the weed-eater. It was bouncing all over the place and going crazy, yet He was laughing and having the best time. As I saw this, my heart softened and I felt Jesus' truth—it is okay to be messy while learning something new, and it doesn't mean I'm "less than" or a failure. What I felt from that picture of Him has been something I recall and hold onto anytime those old beliefs try to sneak their way back into my life.

Sometimes after going through this process, I could literally feel a weight lifted off my shoulders as the lies I'd been believing for so many years dissolved. Other times, I would pray and it was a struggle to feel God or any difference at all, but I did it anyway, knowing that even if the results weren't tangible in that moment, I was still moving toward healing and freedom.

The other battlefront was in my present life and how those old mindsets were coming out in sexual urges, fear of failing my wife, fear of not being good enough for my job, etc. Every time I recognized that a fear I was currently experiencing was due to an old mindset, I would go through the same process: I would repent for the faulty beliefs, ask Him to tell me His truth instead, and then I would do my best to live out the truth He spoke to me. When I dealt with the present issues, it would often bring up past memories that still had a hold on me, and vice-versa. Healing in the present helped heal me in the past, and healing in the past helped heal me in the present. My process didn't look like a one-time fix, but rather a continual process of breaking those old beliefs and inserting God's truth into my life. Even though the degree of freedom I felt after each time of prayer varied from a significant change to an almost unnoticeable change, every time I faced those old beliefs, I was reinforcing in myself that there is a greater truth for my life.

REINFORCING GOD'S TRUTH

EVERY TIME WE SEE OURSELVES REACTING OUT OF OLD PATTERNS OR BELIEFS, IT'S AN OPPORTUNITY TO CREATE GODLY BELIEF SYSTEMS AND PERSPECTIVES FOR OURSELVES.

To actually get free from faulty core beliefs, we have to face them in every area where they pop up in our lives by recognizing them and then inviting God to speak His truth about the situation to us. Most of us have had years of reinforcing the false identities we developed from our past situations and experiences. We need to become just as diligent in reinforcing God's truth about who we are until it begins to replace those faulty beliefs. Every time we see ourselves reacting out of old patterns of beliefs, it's an opportunity not only to fight the lies, but more importantly, to create Godly belief systems and perspectives of ourselves.

We can receive general truths if we are seeking answers on our own, but when we go to God in these areas, He speaks directly to the heart of the issue, allowing us to move forward in the true identity He meant for us to have.

As you begin this process of recognizing core beliefs that were developed from past hurts, pain, and traumas, don't worry if things don't change right away. This is going to be a process that will continue throughout the course of your life. Continue to be willing to go to Him when He brings up new memories or areas where those old habits and beliefs originated, and you will see a deep and meaningful change over time. Stay dependent on Him and watch how well He can heal your past.

Activation

If you are having sexual triggers that seem to pop out of nowhere and you can't find an immediate need or pain you are trying to avoid, there is a good chance the sexual trigger stems from flawed mindsets and belief systems created from your past. If this is true for you:

1. Ask yourself what you think you will be receiving if the temptation were to be fulfilled.
2. Ask God where this faulty belief first came into your life.
3. As God shows you, repent for any ways you've partnered with the faulty belief.
4. Ask God how He sees you or the situation instead of your faulty belief.

As you run into the manifestations of these old mindsets in your relationships, fight for sexual freedom, work habits, or any other area, follow the same process above. If the sexual trigger really does stem from past mindsets created in times of trauma, then it will show up in other areas besides your sexual struggle. The more areas in which you face it, the quicker you will begin to create a Godly mindset.

Sometimes you will get stuck doing this by yourself. In these times, it is essential to call a friend, counselor, or pastor—someone who can help you break old mindsets and hear from God in these areas. Pursuing healing in these deeper issues is going to make a significant difference in your struggle with porn, and the benefits will be felt in many other areas of your life. Make a lifelong commitment never to stop trying to shift your mindset to God's as He brings up faulty belief systems.

Sometimes You're Just Horny

One day when I was working, I noticed I felt a desire for sex that was stronger than normal. This was after two or three months of not looking at porn or masturbating. Instantly, I mentally geared up to prepare for a fight to keep my mind pure, but when I stopped to think of which thoughts or triggers were going through my head, I discovered something weird. There was no trigger, no sexual thoughts, no fantasies, no lust of any kind that I could tell. I was slightly puzzled since I couldn't remember the last time I felt a desire for sex but didn't have some trigger to go along with it.

What I realized through this experience is that I will have times where I am just horny, and that's okay. My body will get to a place where it desires sex and as long as I don't enter into lust or fantasy, it's all right for me to be "horny." It means my body is functioning the way God designed it to function. I will say, there was a tug to start fantasizing or indulging in sexual thoughts as an instant outlet for my elevated sex drive, but instead I thanked God that my sex drive was working and told myself to wait and express this desire later with my wife.

DIFFERENTIATING BETWEEN TRIGGERS AND OUR SEX DRIVE

GOD CREATED US WITH HORMONES AND A SEX DRIVE. IT IS A BEAUTIFUL GIFT THAT IS DESIGNED TO BRING INTIMACY, UNITY, AND BONDING BETWEEN US AND OUR SPOUSE.

As we go through this journey of seeking sexual freedom, it can be easy to fall into the mindset that our sexual desires are the enemy. This is not true. God created us with hormones and a sex drive, and it's a beautiful gift that is designed to bring intimacy, unity, and bonding between us and our spouse. If we ignored it completely in an attempt to try and get free sexually, we would simply be shutting down a part of who we are. That's not God's desire for us, nor should it be ours. Our goal should be to separate our God-given sex drive from our attempts to use porn and sex to meet needs and numb pain that were never meant to be dealt with that way. Abstaining from negative sexual behaviors is only part of the journey toward sexual freedom. The other necessary part is learning how to fully embrace our sex drive and manage it in a healthy way.

When everything is working the way it is supposed to, we will have days when our sex drive is higher and we want sex more. While we are detangling ourselves from all the images, fantasies, and lustful views of sex, the days we have a higher sex drive may feel like just another sexual trigger—but they aren't. It is important for us to learn how to differentiate between a healthy sex drive and an unhealthy sexual trigger. Being able to tell the difference will allow us to fully embrace the gift God gave us while not furthering the inaccurate and unhealthy view of sex created by porn.

HOW TO TELL THE DIFFERENCE

A sexual trigger usually has a strong pull to be met instantly through porn or sexualization, but the trigger itself isn't sexual in nature. An example of this is wanting to look at a woman and sexually fantasize about her because you are bored in life and want to feel excited. You may think this is your sex drive since you have a strong desire to look at a woman in a sexual way, but it is really a need for excitement and adventure you are trying to meet through sexualizing. On the other hand, if you feel like you want sex but it hasn't originated from a stimulus—a woman you saw, sexual thoughts you indulged, or some other need trying to be met via sexualizing—it is a pretty good indicator that your sex drive is just operating a bit higher at that moment.

The tricky part is having self-control and not allowing your natural sex drive to turn into an excuse for indulging in sexual urges. When you are horny, your natural response is to seek fulfillment and release of the sexual tension. If all you've known is the use of sex as an instant-gratification tool to make yourself feel better, it will probably

> EVERY TIME YOU INDULGE IN AN UNHEALTHY SEXUAL URGE WHEN YOU HAVE A HIGHER LIBIDO, YOU ARE TRAINING YOURSELF TO PAIR YOUR NATURAL SEX DRIVE WITH LUST.

be what you are tempted to do when experiencing a higher sex drive. Every time you indulge in an unhealthy sexual urge when you have a higher libido, you are training yourself to pair your natural sex drive with lust. Operating in lust is when you use sex for needs it was never meant to fulfill. On the contrary, when you are able to use self-control and not indulge in porn or sexual fantasy to meet your needs, you are learning how to embrace your sex drive, and at the same time, manage it in a healthy way.

What most people, and especially singles, don't realize is that learning how to manage your sex drive is one of the keys to having an amazing sex life when you are married. When you are using sex to meet needs it wasn't designed to meet, it will never satisfy, even when it's with your spouse. Learning how to engage in sex with your spouse for the sake of genuine intimacy and connection allows for the most passionate and expressive sex, because it is utilizing sex in the way God intended it to be used.

WHAT TO DO WHEN YOU ARE HORNY AND SINGLE

What I felt when I was single and what I heard from many other singles' mouths is the question, "How can I manage my sex drive when I don't have a spouse to have sex with?" This question is usually followed by, "Is it wrong to masturbate to manage my sex drive?" I don't actually like the phrase, "Is it wrong?" because it oversimplifies a complex issue and takes away the awareness of consequences. We all have the freedom of choice. If we want to, we can choose to masturbate whenever we want, but there are consequences for how we use our sexuality. Hopefully the reason we are trying to seek sexual freedom isn't simply because it is "right" or "wrong," but because we've seen the damaging effects it has on our lives and want more than what unhealthy sexualization in any form has given us. If you are lusting and fantasizing while masturbating, you are fueling the same dependency on sexualization that porn creates.

I also often get asked questions like, "What if I'm not fantasizing while I'm masturbating?" Or, "What if I don't masturbate very often? Is it still unhealthy?" I don't have a direct answer to these questions, but I will say that I have never heard of masturbation being beneficial for someone who is recovering from porn or someone who has used sexualization to distract themselves from pain in their lives. Masturbating in these contexts almost always leads deeper down the rabbit hole and opens doors to the use of sexuality in an unhealthy way.

These questions often arise as a result of feeling like it is too difficult to manage your sex drive. One way to make managing your sex drive easier is by healthily meeting the other areas of needs in your life (health, sleep, job, connection with God, connection with family and friends, etc.). When we aren't meeting one or more of our core needs, it puts a strain on the rest of our needs to make up the slack. For some singles, managing their sex drive feels nearly impossible. Many times this is the result of having multiple unmet needs. The more you take care of your other needs, the less overwhelmed you will feel in this area when employing self-control.

For those of you who are single and are asking yourself why you should learn how to manage your sex drive before you are married, the answer is that you have two choices. You can either begin preparing for great sex in your marriage now, or you can continue to create unhealthy habits that you will bring into your marriage, making what is meant to be one of the most pleasurable and bonding acts in your marriage a dissatisfying, isolating action to illegitimately get your needs met.

WHAT TO DO WHEN YOU ARE HORNY AND MARRIED

It's a common belief that you no longer need self-control or a healthy management of your sex drive when you are married. This is very far from the truth. In some ways, even more self-control is required in marriage. Sex is an extremely powerful and bonding act. We have a strong, innate desire for it, and yet it requires another person. We cannot fulfill our sex drive in the way God intended apart from relationship with our spouse. When we feel horny, instead of looking at it as a personal need we need to selfishly fulfill, we should think of it as an "internal clock" God gave us to pursue and intimately connect with our spouse. Having a healthy marriage relationship is very important to God, and our sex drive is just one of the ways He helps us be intentional about maintaining our connection and intimacy.

To really enjoy sex to the fullest and allow it to be all that God intended it to be, we can't be saddling it with needs it was never meant to fulfill. Allow your sex drive to remain a gift for your spouse for the purpose of bringing deeper intimacy and bonding. Let it be something that is only meant to be expressed between the two of you.

One of the most powerful prayers I have prayed, and continued to pray on my journey in seeking sexual wholeness, is: "God, continue to show me how you see sex and sexuality instead of what I've learned from porn and media." We can always receive deeper revelations about the beauty and gift of sex if we seek God's truth. As we understand the original intent of our sex drive from God's perspective, it becomes that much easier to want to use it in the way He designed.

Activation

If you feel an increased desire for sex, stop and try to recognize how much of it may be your God-given sex drive and how much of it maybe unhealthy sexualization. In the beginning, it may help to rate your sex drive on a scale of 1 to 10 each day just to better familiarize yourself with your body.

Managing your sex drive becomes increasingly difficult when other areas of your life aren't being managed well. Here is a list of areas in your life you should check on regularly:

1. **SPIRITUALLY:** How is your connection with God? Do you feel close to Him?

2. **EMOTIONALLY:** What kind of emotions have you been feeling lately? If they tend to be uncomfortable emotions, how are they being managed? Have you had alone time to process your emotions?

3. **PHYSICALLY:** Are you getting plenty of rest? Are you taking care of your physical body through movement and exercise? What kind of foods have you been feeding your body? Are they healthy, higher-quality foods or are they low-quality processed foods?

4. **RELATIONALLY:** How are you doing in your
    relationships with others? Do you feel connected
    to them? Do you feel seen and understood in
    those relationships? Are you pursuing others
    in relationships?

If and when your sex drive feels out of control, go over this list as many times as you need and find out how you are doing in each of these areas.

Commit to becoming a student of how God views sexuality. We need to re-educate ourselves with how He sees it versus how the world sees it. Sex is a good thing that God Himself created, but sometimes we can forget this and become too embarrassed or ashamed to bring Him into this area of our lives. Ask Him this every morning when you wake up: "God, will You restore my views of sexuality so they are aligned with Your views of sexuality? I give You complete permission to change any views or beliefs I have of sex that don't line up with how You see it."

Make Your Life More Attractive Than Porn

While I have gained significant levels of breakthrough on my journey of freedom from porn, honestly there are still some days when porn sounds attractive to me, where it seems like it will make me feel loved and comforted. Luckily on those days, I have my willpower to help me make smart decisions even when my emotions don't line up. But I don't want to stay in the place where I am solely relying on my willpower.

Our lives need to become more appealing to us than porn, so that our emotions actually line up with the desire for sexual freedom. I believe there will always be times when we need to exercise our willpower, but our goal should be to have our emotions on our side, pushing us toward healthy sexuality the majority of the time. Achieving this goal will not happen simply from praying right in the middle of temptations, even though those are necessary steps. It only occurs with an actual lifestyle shift.

> **OUR LIVES NEED TO BECOME MORE APPEALING TO US THAN PORN, SO THAT OUR EMOTIONS ACTUALLY LINE UP WITH THE DESIRE FOR SEXUAL FREEDOM.**

So the question is, how do we create a shift to make our lives more attractive than porn? The answer lies in discovering our passions, risk-taking, and utilizing discipline to live the adventurous, fulfilling life God designed for us.

THE PASSIONS WITHIN

To develop an attractive life, we have to first discover what we are passionate about. Unfortunately, as porn users, we have developed an instant-gratification mindset, which has detached us from those passions and replaced them with compulsions. Our passions are connected to our dreams and desires, but after years of ignoring them by checking out with sexualizing and fillers, we have to be intentional to reconnect ourselves with our dormant passions.

When I first stopped looking at porn, I couldn't think of anything that I thought was more exciting than pornography. I had forgotten my passions, and with that, my ability to live a truly fulfilling life. Luckily, as I continued on in my sobriety, my passions slowly began coming back to me, and with them came a whole new world of facing fears, accomplishing goals, and feeling alive in ways an instant-gratification lifestyle never made me feel.

One of the first passions that came back to me was my desire to make a difference in the world by bringing wholeness and restoration to people's lives. A way I aspired to accomplish this was through writing blogs and books. Unfortunately, in the beginning this desire never seemed to come to fruition. My writing career looked like a whole lot of procrastination, evasion, and excuses. Every time I thought about sitting down to write, I would get hit with ten different fears all at once: *I'm not good enough. I'm going to sound stupid. I'm going to find out I can't do what I love.* As these waves of anxiety hit, my habit of avoidance would kick in and I would let my passions pass me by. I couldn't even follow through with the desires of my heart that were meant to bring me life. I was enslaved by the whims of what I felt moment by moment, and it was causing me to be a bystander in my own life. I knew something needed to change. Otherwise, no matter how much I was able to abstain from sexual sin and other fillers, my life would still end up feeling empty and purposeless.

I began with setting some realistic goals I knew I could follow through with. In the past I had been an "all or nothing" guy. I would go from one extreme of having absolutely no goals or aspirations to making ridiculous goals that I had no hope of maintaining without burning out. This pattern was a remnant of my instant-gratification lifestyle and attempts to make change instantaneous. So this time around, I took time to process and think about what a realistic aim for myself would be, and came up with a small writing goal I knew I could maintain. I decided that two days a week I would write for an hour in the morning before work. It seemed small, but that was the point. My goal wasn't simply to write; it was to restore confidence in my ability to follow through with my choice regardless of what I felt in the moment, which would ultimately move me toward living in my passion.

Even though I was writing only two hours a week, I still got hit with all those same fears when it came time to write. I made myself persevere anyway. I won't lie—facing those fears didn't always feel good. There were times I really wanted to stop early or skip my writing time all together, but I didn't. Despite my fears, I moved forward, and the more I pushed toward this goal, the better I felt about myself and the direction of my life overall.

PURSUING PASSIONS BRINGS LIFE VISION

I can't tell you how good it felt to be able to follow through with something I was passionate about, even in the midst of fear and opposition. It made me feel alive and powerful. We all have many passions inside us, ranging from big dreams to smaller fun experiences. There is a proverb that says, "Hope deferred makes the heart sick, but a dream fulfilled is a tree of life" (Proverbs 13:12 NLT). During the porn addiction stage, we experienced our heart being sick plenty of times as we ignored our passions and let our forgotten dreams pass us by. Now is the time for us to experience the "tree of life" stage as we boldly pursue the passions God has given us.

It's time to ask yourself, "What am I passionate about? What do I have a genuine longing for?" These questions can be tough to answer, especially if we are used to having our "wants" drowned out with "shoulds." When we are asked what we are passionate about, do we respond with what we think is the "right" or "acceptable" answer, or do we respond authentically? Our passions have to come from our *own* heart and emotions. They can't stem from "shoulds" or what we think others would want us to be passionate about.

Spend some time rediscovering your passions and write them down. Whether you are passionate about listening to music while out in nature or writing a New York Times bestseller, the important thing is that your passions are genuinely connected to your heart. When you start reopening the gate to your lost desires and experiencing your passions fulfilled firsthand, it will lead to the discovery of even deeper passions God has placed inside you.

As you begin connecting to the passions of your heart, those passions will often morph into a bigger vision for your life. Having vision for your life means that you have direction, purpose, and clear knowledge of the kind of life you want to live and the kind of person you want to be. It is important to be able to discover your life vision— otherwise you will be wasting time and energy on things like porn and sexualizing that aren't connected to your heart's desire or passions.

Having a vision helps show you where to spend your time so that you are effectively living a life that makes you come alive. This doesn't mean you'll have all the answers by any means. We are continually changing, getting new passions and vision for our life. But it does mean

> **HAVING A VISION HELPS SHOW YOU WHERE TO SPEND YOUR TIME SO THAT YOU ARE EFFECTIVELY LIVING A LIFE THAT MAKES YOU COME ALIVE.**

we have an intentional direction in which we are moving. Fulfilling the various passions in our life is highly life-giving and motivational, but it is only the beginning.

God created us well. As we follow the genuine passions He has placed inside us and begin creating vision for our lives, our focus shifts from survival mode and avoiding pain to carrying out our dreams, which brings meaning and purpose to our lives.

FACING CHALLENGES AND RUNNING AT YOUR FEARS

As I started giving a voice to my dormant passions and taking steps toward living them out, additional passions began to spring up in other areas of my life. Despite the challenges that came with these new passions, I began taking risks to bring them to life. I started life coaching—something I had cared about for a long time but was previously too afraid to step into. I stuck to a weekly workout routine to move me toward my passion of having a healthy body. I challenged myself to share more openly with my wife when I felt hurt, which I used to avoid, in order to move me toward my passion of having a deep, intimate connection with her. I also increased my writing and blogging routine to every weekday. I received two promotions at my job—both of which carried more responsibility and authority, which terrified me, yet I ran toward these opportunities. In many different areas of my life, I was saying "yes" to challenges, and I was able to follow through. Being able to choose my vision over my fears and negative feelings became exhilarating. I was blown away with how taking courageous risks to pursue my life vision was making life so enjoyable.

Part of the thrill of pursuing your passions and creating vision for your life is finding out you can overcome the fears and challenges that arise along the way. As you pursue your passions, you will encounter challenges and risks, as well as failures. That is simply a part of life, and it is actually what makes achieving victory in our goals so life-giving. It brings a strong sense of accomplishment. I used to be addicted to instant gratification, which never satisfied me, challenged me, or pushed me into my destiny. I now feel the same desire for taking risks and facing challenges that I used to feel for instant gratification, except the payoff is much better. As a result of running at my fears, I am enjoying my life much more, and I'm continually growing and challenging myself while living a life of which I feel proud.

If you don't have bigger passions for your life yet, start with simply running at your fears. As you persevere through the hardships, I guarantee you will begin to feel a difference in the desirability of your life. As you progress, continually ask yourself, "What do I want my life to look like?" The goal is to make your life purposeful, fun, and attractive. As you do, your desire to check out with porn and other fillers will decrease.

DISCIPLINE MAKES YOUR VISION HAPPEN

There is another element needed to help us choose the courageous path through challenges and risks in order to turn our dreams into reality. That element is *discipline*. That word used to be a huge turn-off for me. Growing up, I often thought those who lived disciplined lives had boring lives. Through my journey toward freedom, I've found it to be quite the opposite. Discipline is actually the gateway to a free and fulfilling life. *When discipline isn't present, you end up becoming a slave to your emotions*, yet implementing discipline in your life is what makes living out your dreams possible.

So what does discipline actually look like? Discipline is about creating systems to make it as easy as possible to continually move toward your vision—not just for a temporary period of time, but throughout the course of your life. It is easy to face challenges for a moment, a day, or even a few weeks, but few of us are able to make it a lifestyle because we often let laziness, tiredness, stress, fear, etc. guide our choices. These are the times when implementing discipline is key. Exercising our discipline "muscle" helps make choosing what's best for us become more automatic and less of an emotional response. This sets us up to reap the benefits of making the best choice, even though we may not feel the benefits of that choice immediately. Over time, however, our lives will become more and more fulfilling in a sustainable way as discipline becomes a lifestyle.

Here's another way to look at it: When I used to read the Bible or try to spend time with God, if I didn't feel His presence right away or get some deep revelation, I would always assume I had done something wrong. I expected to see instant rewards for my efforts and I based my success upon whether or not those rewards were present. As a result, I was stuck in a cycle of regaining hope to try again, feeling disappointment, feeling like a failure, and then giving up.

As I started learning about the importance of discipline

and vision in my life, I began to see things differently. I thought about it like physically working out. If you choose to work out your body for a couple of days, you will see very little change in your physique. If you want to see change in your body, you need to work out consistently to get all the benefits. The results will be gradual but deep-rooted—increased health, stronger cardiovascular system, stronger muscles, better self-esteem, fewer illnesses, etc. All these benefits happen just from continuing to persevere when the results aren't instantaneous. The benefits of choosing discipline over instant gratification are always deeper and longer lasting.

I began looking at other disciplines in my life, such as reading the Bible and spending time with God, in the same way I looked at physically working out. I knew I wanted the benefits of having a strong and rich spiritual life, so I needed to put the time and effort into connecting with God if I wanted to see that deeper lifestyle change. I caught the greater vision and all the benefits I would gain by having spiritual discipline in my life. This motivation created excitement in me to pursue this area, even knowing the rewards wouldn't be instantaneous. It allowed me to be satisfied with steady goals that I knew would keep me moving in the right direction.

BABY STEPS

Discipline is the key to living a continuously passionate lifestyle. And the key to discipline is creating small, achievable goals. The point of a goal is to create small stepping stones toward a grander purpose that otherwise couldn't be accomplished without breaking it up into pieces. Have you ever started an extreme diet and quit after a couple weeks? Have you ever made a workout goal that you weren't able to maintain? I certainly have, and it was usually because I was making my goal too big in an attempt to experience the benefits right away, without the discipline needed to make it a lifestyle change. When our goals are too big or unrealistic, it's an indicator that we are still searching for an instant change. By creating small goals we can maintain, like my two-hour-per-week writing goal, we get to take small but more permanent steps toward the life we want to be living.

WHEN OUR GOALS ARE TOO BIG OR UNREALISTIC, IT'S AN INDICATOR THAT WE ARE STILL SEARCHING FOR INSTANT CHANGE.

Another example of a small goal I created was attached to my desire to feel productive and accomplished after a day of work. My problem was that sometimes I would run out of tasks to do in my position and I would end up not knowing how to spend the rest of my work time. So I created a goal of writing out my work schedule every morning, including some things I could work on if I finished early. This made all the difference for me. At the end of the day, I could see all that I had accomplished, and I no longer felt directionless if I finished my tasks early, since I had created a plan earlier. The small choice to write out my schedule every morning allowed me to come home from work feeling accomplished, which added to my overall quality of life.

Life isn't a sprint—it's a marathon. Forward movement is good, even if the steps are smaller than you originally expected. This is how you create a lifestyle change.

THE NON-NEGOTIABLES

In my life, I discovered some fundamental areas where I needed to create goals to make sure they were getting the attention they deserved. When I didn't put focus into these sections of my life, I could feel my overall life quality drop, and soon the desire for an instant-gratification "fix," like porn, would resurface. These main areas were:

- SPIRITUAL HEALTH
- PHYSICAL HEALTH
- RELATIONSHIPS (WITH SPOUSE AND CLOSE COMMUNITY OF FRIENDS AND FAMILY)
- JOB/CAREER
- SEXUAL HEALTH/SEXUALITY
- FUN & RECREATION
- REST & RELAXATION

In every one of these categories, I asked myself what I wanted my life to look like, and began creating small goals that moved me one step closer toward my overall life vision. Each of these categories can be broken down further into smaller subcategories, all of which can have their own smaller goals, but in my experience these all deserve special attention. Otherwise, continued healthy functionality will become increasingly difficult.

Activation

Create an ongoing list where you can write down all of your passions and dreams, no matter how seemingly big or small. Make sure to keep it so you can add to it as time goes on.

In each of the following categories, begin writing down a vision for what you want your life to look like:

- **SPIRITUAL HEALTH**
- **PHYSICAL HEALTH**
- **RELATIONSHIPS (WITH SPOUSE AND CLOSE COMMUNITY OF FRIENDS AND FAMILY)**
- **JOB/CAREER**
- **SEXUAL HEALTH/SEXUALITY**
- **FUN & RECREATION**
- **REST & RELAXATION**

As you come up with your vision for each of these areas, write down small, achievable, and specific goals under each category, which will help you move toward your overall life vision. Once you have written them down, choose only 2—3 goals to begin working on at a time. Working on only 2—3 goals at a time will help prevent you from feeling overwhelmed and possibly quitting altogether as a result.

As those 2—3 goals are being achieved sustainably in your life, you can begin adding more.

I highly encourage you to share your goals with someone else, such as your spouse, a friend, or a family member. Sharing your goals with other people greatly increases the likelihood of you staying committed to achieving them.

Remember, your aim is to seek continual, sustainable growth in your life, not an instant change.

CONCLUSION

Throughout my journey, I have continually needed to remind myself of the values and lessons I've learned as I've pursued sexual wholeness. For example, there were times in my process where I got lax about sharing my "small" struggles, and I had to remind myself how important it was to let others into my life and live with nothing hidden. Other times, I would find myself sliding back into managing my temptations, and I would have to recalibrate by inviting God into those temptations and allowing Him to speak to me. For my continued progress, reflection on what God has previously shown me has been vital.

I tell you this because I believe it will be necessary for you to do the same thing. Remember that the goal isn't to have a perfect process without hiccups. It's okay if you've slid off track a bit, as long as you stay humble, give yourself grace, and regain focus.

The insights and steps you've gained through this book and through your personal journey toward sexual wholeness are invaluable. They will help you not only to maintain the progress you've made; they have also laid a firm foundation for you to continue to grow. Regularly go back through this book and remind yourself of the steps that have helped bring you breakthrough on your journey. Ask yourself if you are continuing to pursue your vision of the kind of person you want to be and the kind of life you want to live.

As best as you can, continue to hold close to your heart the gravity and importance of:

- Sexual purity
- Living life vulnerably in community
- Taking ownership of your mistakes
- Courageously facing and moving through your pain
- Inviting God right into the middle of temptations
- Inviting God into past hurts to bring restoration
- Fully embracing your God-given sexuality in a healthy way
- Learning to live a disciplined, purposeful, and fulfilling life

As you maintain these foundational core values for seeking sexual purity, you will see how these same core values vastly improve and enhance your life in all areas.

God is raising us up from the ashes of sexual brokenness to lead, not only in sexual purity, but in how to live powerful and influential lives in humility and dependency on Him. We no longer have to look on our past with shame. Instead, we get to marvel at how much God has changed us and used something that brought so much pain and torment in our lives as a catalyst to make us stronger than ever before. I'm proud of you for going on this journey, and I know God is too.

ACKNOWLEDGEMENTS

First and foremost, I want to thank my beautiful, incredible, heart-stopping wife—Katie Byrne. Without you, this book would not exist. Thank you for your willingness to get down and dirty by going on this journey of wholeness with me. It has meant the world to me to have had you by my side through the thick and thin of this process. Your patience, understanding, wisdom, and most incredibly, your unconditional love has made me marvel at the caliber of woman God made you to be, and has been an indispensible strength for me during this journey. Thank you for showing me a whole new level of what Godly love looks like and being such a voice of encouragement to share my journey with others.

Mark Peterson and all the men from the Purity Pursuit group—thank you for teaching me what brutal honesty looks like and giving me a safe place to be fully known. You all have been there for me every step of the way.

Dad, thank you for being such a humble and caring father. You loved me in such a deep way every time you chose to go into those places of pain with me to help me mend and to help our relationship grow even stronger. You truly are my role model.

Mom, thank you for being my biggest fan. Your optimism and hope for my life and this book have been contagious. Thanks for always being in my corner.

Justin Stumvoll and Andy Flaherty, thank you for your guidance and coaching during the times I really needed it.

God, thank You for Your eternal love and gift of redemption through Jesus. I, and every other person who has messed up, still get to live in Your goodness because You gave your Son for us. Thank You for giving us all the hope of life.

MORE INFORMATION

For more information about Brendon Byrne's
products, services, resources, and itinerary,
please visit his website at
www.brendonbyrne.com.